Victoria's Golden Jubilee

THE BRITISH LION PREPARES FOR THE JUBILEE.

Frontispiece
The British Lion prepares for the Jubilee

Punch magazine published this cartoon on 18 June 1887, when the public were beginning to look forward to the forthcoming festivities, and to realise the extent of the celebrations.

VICTORIA'S GOLDEN JUBILEE

JOHN FABB

Seaby
London

© John Fabb 1987
First published 1987

Typeset by Tek Art Ltd, Kent
and printed and bound in Great Britain
by Butler & Tanner Ltd.
Frome, Somerset
for the publishers
B.A. Seaby Ltd
8 Cavendish Square,
London W1M 0AJ

Distributed by
B.T. Batsford Ltd.
P.O. Box 4, Braintree, Essex CM7 7QY

ISBN 0 900652 95 0

CONTENTS

ACKNOWLEDGMENTS

The author and publishers would like to thank the following for permission to reproduce copyright illustrations:

Punch Magazine   *1, 53, 71*

The British Library   *23, 24, 26-8*

Hawaiian National Archives   *30-33*

Guildhall Library   *34-8, 43-6, 48*

BBC Hulton Picture Library   *39, 40, 42, 79, 80*

B.T. Batsford Ltd   *47, 57-64, 76-8, 91, 99*

Hampshire County Museum Service   *65*

Royal Borough of Kensington and Chelsea Libraries and Art Service *66-70*

Greenwich Picture Library   *81-90*

National Army Museum, London   *92*

National Portrait Gallery, London   *93-7*

Buffalo Bill Historical Center, Wyoming   *98*

Metropolitan Police, London   *100*

Bodleian Library, Oxford (Per. 256d 253)   *101*

Reproduced by gracious permission of Her Majesty the Queen   *2-22, 25, 29, 49, 54-6*

The remaining photographs were provided by the author.

INTRODUCTION

The Royal Jubilee 1887

The idea of a Golden Jubilee appealed both to the public and to Parliament. The Queen's insistence on not appearing in public except when unavoidable had not improved the image of the royal family. Republican clubs had been formed up and down the country, and although they were small in number, Parliament was concerned. It was necessary for the Queen to be seen in public, and the Jubilee would be a chance to demonstrate that this was the largest and mightiest Empire on earth. The Prince of Wales first aroused the Queen's interest in the Jubilee and plans were laid for one of the largest family gatherings of all time. The Queen gradually became more interested in the preparations, and began by insisting that Court regulations be modified at her Drawing-rooms to admit ladies who had been innocent parties in divorce cases. She later asked the Prime Minister, Lord Salisbury, if innocent foreign ladies might also be admitted. He advised against it, because of the risk of admitting American women of light character.

Congratulations were sent from all over the Empire to the Queen and Empress. Prisoners were released from jail, and in a burst of celebration at Mithi in India, the 'Queen Victoria's Jubilee Burial and Burning Ground' was opened. In Singapore extra rice rations were given to hospital patients, as well as to lepers, who wished Her Majesty a reign of ten thousand years.

Before the rigours of the Jubilee celebrations the Queen took a holiday in the South of France at Cannes and Aix-les-Bains. It was the first time that the Queen had visited Aix, and she was so much taken with the place that she considered buying a villa there.

A short distance away was Chambery, the headquarters of the French Army Alpine Corps. With typical French courtesy the President insisted that the most charming and accomplished officers were selected to command the guard of honour at the Queen's villa.

There had been no similar ceremony since the Jubilee of King George III on 25 October 1809. The country was then at war with France and cut off from Europe, so that particular celebration could not form a precedent for Queen Victoria's Jubilee. Consequently, the arrangements for the Jubilee of 1887 had to be made without the benefit of any previous experience. The Prince of Wales was the instigator, and arranged the details for the whole function with the Queen's advisors. It was the Prince who met all the foreign royalty as they arrived, and arranged their accommodation in various palaces according to rank and precedence.

On 17 May the Queen visited the East End of London. When she opened the People's Palace in the Mile End Road, large crowds gathered to see their recluse of a Queen and welcomed her enthusiastically. However, the Queen did become aware of a disagreeable noise, which was, as the Prime Minister informed her, 'booing, as it is called'. He explained that it was only the Socialists or, at worst, the Irish.

After her usual stay at Balmoral in Scotland, the Queen journeyed south. Throughout the country she was received with wild enthusiasm and began to realise the esteem in which she was held by the British people. At Windsor Castle the Queen rested and prepared for the great day. On 20 June she left for London. Dressed in black, she was driven to Buckingham Palace in a plain four-horse landau. As soon as the Queen was recognized by the crowds that already thronged the streets, there were tremendous outbursts of cheering and waving – a foretaste of things to come.

All through the night the crowds sang and danced. By morning the Mall outside the Palace was a sea of faces, not only Londoners but tens of thousands of people from the provinces and all over the Empire. The route of the procession was lined with crowds before daybreak. Outside Buckingham Palace the broad courtyard inside the railings was filled with cavalry, whose helmets and sabres flashed and glittered in the early morning sun. At ten o'clock, Prince George, Duke of Cambridge rode up to the Palace from Whitehall, with the military staff. At eleven o'clock, a fanfare of trumpets from the Life Guards made heads turn towards the entrance of Buckingham Palace.

First came an advance party of the First Life Guards, then came aide-de-camps and equerries, representatives of the volunteer forces that included the Duke of Westminster. Then the crowds could see the first of the cream-coloured Hanoverian horses swinging into view. A tumultuous roar broke forth as the small figure sitting in the coach was recognised. The Queen had obstinately refused to wear the crown and robes, insisting that she would wear her usual black costume and bonnet or she would not go. However, at least she wore a special bonnet of white lace decorated with diamonds. As the guard of honour crashed to the present arms, the bands broke into the national anthem and the Queen's entourage swept out of the palace gates to join the procession. The Prince of Wales had organised the huge ceremonial procession into three parts. The first section was formed up in Hyde Park, while the remainder moved in after the Queen's party had left Buckingham Palace.

Certain of the royal guests were sent on ahead to Westminster Abbey, to await the coming of the Queen. All arrivals were scheduled, so that the junior members of the royal family entered the Abbey at 10.20 precisely. These were Princess Feodore of Saxe-Meiningen, Prince Albert and Princess Louise of Schleswig-Holstein-Sonderburg-Augustenburg, Princess Alix of Hesse and By Rhine, and the daughters of Prince Alfred, Duke of Edinburgh. Ten minutes later arrived Baron and Baroness von Pawel Rammingen. The baroness was a daughter of King George of Hanover. Prince Edward of Saxe-Weimar-Eisenach, the Prince and Princess of Leiningen, Count and Countess Gleichen and Prince and Princess Victor of Hohenlohe-Langenburg followed in their turn. Meanwhile the procession was winding its way through the streets of London, headed by distinguished Indian princes and deputations from the Indian states. The Maharajah of Cooch Bihar, the Maharao of Kutch and the Maharajah Holkar of Indore headed this distinguished and brilliant company. Next came the Thakor of Gondal, the Thakor of Limbdi and the Maharajah of Morvi, who was at this time receiving an annual income of four million pounds. The Indian noblemen of states not represented by their rulers brought up the end of this part of the procession. These states included such famous names as Hyderabad, Alwar, Jodpure, Bhurtapore and Kapurthala. In the open carriages were the family of the Duke and Duchess of Teck, including Princess Mary of Teck, soon to be engaged to the heir to the throne, Prince Albert Victor, Duke of Clarence and Avondale. The third section of the procession was composed of Queen Victoria's other guests. These were the representatives of the Shah of Persia, Prince Devawongse of Siam, the Crown Prince of Japan, Queen Kapiolani of Hawaii, and her daughter, Princess Liliuokalani.

Preceeding the Queen were representatives of those royal houses of Europe with which the English Crown had a special affinity or friendship. These were the kings of Belgium, Denmark, Greece and Saxony; the Crown Princes of Austria, Greece, Portugal and Sweden; Prince Ludwig of Bavaria; Prince Philip of Saxe-Coburg-Gotha; the Grand Duke and Duchess of Mecklenburg-Strelitz; the Prince of Hohenlohe-Langenburg, and the family of the Prince of Saxe-Weimar-Eisenach. Of particular interest to the crowds was a special guard of honour accompanying the royal carriage, composed of the sons, grandsons, sons-in-law, and grand-sons-in-law of Queen Victoria. This party was led by the Queen's sons: Edward Prince of Wales, Prince Arthur Duke of Connaught and Strathearn, and Prince Alfred Duke of Edinburgh. Grand Duke Sergei of Russia led the rest of the family; namely Crown Prince Friedrich, Prince Heinrich and Prince Wilhelm of Prussia; Prince Louis and Prince Henry of Battenberg; Prince Christian Viktor of Schleswig-Holstein-Sonderburg-Augustenburg, and Ludwig IV, Grand Duke of Hesse and By Rhine and his son Prince Ernst. Next came the two sons of the Prince of Wales, Prince Albert Victor, Duke of Clarence and Avondale, and Prince George, and finally John Campbell, Marquis of Lorne.

As the Queen proceeded along the route, her reception was tumultuous. The music played by the military bands could hardly be heard above the roar of the crowds. The procession was brought up by a contingent of Indian cavalry and an escort of the First Life Guards.

Inside the Abbey the guests had gradually been arriving since nine o'clock. The hushed building was filled with brilliant colour: provincial Lord Mayors in their red robes, Lord Lieutenants, sheriffs, professors and doctors in court dress. Later came the foreign ambassadors, the peers and peeresses, the judiciary and members of the House of Commons. The jewellery of the ladies and also of the Indian princes and their suites sparkled in the sombre Abbey. A fanfare of trumpets broke the silence and the great doors were flung open wide. Slowly the Queen walked in, clothed in black, relieved only by the Orders of the Garter and the Star of India. The organ played one of Handel's Marches as the Queen was followed by the clergy and the royal heralds in their tabards. Behind the Queen's party came the Prince of Wales and the other royal princes. When the Queen was seated the congregation gave thanks, the choir sang and the royal family embraced the Queen. Then they returned to the palace in a repetition of the morning's drive, with cheering crowds all the way along to the gates of Buckingham Palace. Luncheon began at four, followed by a march past of the Royal Navy, which the Queen watched from the balcony. At dinner that night the Queen wore a special gown embroidered with silver roses, thistles, and shamrocks. After receiving the ambassadors and Indian princes, the Queen retired at ten o'clock. While Queen Victoria slept, exhausted by the day's events, her guests watched the largest-ever display of fireworks and illuminations over the great city.

On the following day some 30,000 poor children of London gathered in Hyde Park, where each child received a paper bag containing a meat pie, a piece of cake, a bun and an orange, together with a commemorative token. Thousands of shrill young voices greeted the Prince and Princess of Wales as they arrived. Meanwhile the Queen had retired to Windsor Castle to gather her strength for the final Jubilee ceremonies.

On 29 June the Queen returned to London, and three days later reviewed 24,000 army volunteers in Hyde Park in a heat-wave. Then she returned to Windsor, "too exhausted to do anything but rest on a sofa", as her journal records. On 9 July the Queen reviewed the army at Aldershot; some 60,000 men and horses swept past the royal party. Dust blew in the hot summer air as regiment upon regiment passed the Queen in review. Two weeks later, the last and perhaps the grandest of all the Jubilee celebrations took place – the review of the Grand Fleet at Spithead, the largest and most powerful fleet in the world. Some 35 capital ships, 38 gunboats, 43 torpedo boats, and 12 troopships were gathered in lanes through which the royal yacht passed. Twenty thousand sailors cheered their Queen as she returned to Osborne, her retreat on the Isle of Wight. It was so hot at this time that at dinner a huge block of ice stood in the centre of the Queen's dining table. There was an elaborate farewell to the Indian princes and her other private guests, before the Queen herself left for the peace and quiet of the Highlands and her beloved Balmoral Castle.

So ended the Queen's part in the Jubilee, but London was not the only place to honour the Queen with a great show of loyalty to the throne. The usual ox was roasted in several towns, and there were many firework displays and bonfires. Processions and church services were also held. In Manchester, children were treated to breakfast; in Birmingham, brass bands played all day and dinner was given to 3,000 of the aged poor. A special table was included for those of 90 years or older. The local gentry assisted in the serving in many cases, and even the inmates of the workhouse and the asylums were treated to a Christmas-style dinner. In Liverpool, 10,000 trade union members marched through the decorated streets with brass bands playing and banners flying, and all night the city was thronged with dancing crowds. Every hamlet was en fête for this special day.

Abroad, the Queen's Jubilee was celebrated with equal fervour. In the United States, a special service held at Trinity Church in New York was crowded and thousands stood outside. The sermon was "A woman who fears God shall be praised". Flags were flown from all the principal buildings and the ships in the harbour were dressed overall. A great firework display ended the day. Banquets were given in Chicago and Boston, and in Berlin church services and a great banquet were held in the Queen's honour. In St Petersburg, the embassy gave a great reception for the diplomatic corps, but no Russian official attended. Paris was much more exuberant, with dinners for the children and the poor, flags flying from all the buildings, and a thousand free seats at the Hippodrome in honour of the Jubilee. In Vienna, a reception was held by the ambassador, while in Rome a garden party was attended by the whole diplomatic corps and the most noble society of Rome.

The loyalty and love displayed by the people surprised Queen Victoria and never again did she return to the seclusion of previous years. The Golden Jubilee had been a great success and had restored the monarchy to its rightful place in the hearts of the British people. Queen Victoria was to live and reign for another fourteen years, and to celebrate her Diamond Jubilee in 1897, with another spectacular display of loyalty to the British Crown and the Queen and Empress herself.

Politics in Britain

The year of 1887 found the government in the hands of the Conservatives with their allies the Liberal Unionists, led by Prime Minister Robert Cecil, Third Marquess of Salisbury. His deputy and Leader of the House of Commons was Lord Randolph Churchill, whose American-born wife Jennie was a leading Society beauty, together with Lillie Langtry and Georgiana Countess of Dudley, both friends of the Prince of Wales. The Opposition in Parliament was led by the previous year's Prime Minister, William Ewart Gladstone, Leader of the Liberal Party. Queen Victoria could not abide him and was always pleased to see him out of office. The great question of the year was again that of Home Rule for Ireland, which had caused the fall of Gladstone's government in the previous year. The great Irish Nationalist leader was Charles Stewart Parnell, who had taken up the question of Home Rule in 1877. His great aim was to set up an independent Parliament in Dublin. A land owner and a Protestant, he became the most powerful personality in Irish politics since O'Connell.

The armed forces

The Empire was enjoying a rare peace in Jubilee year. The army had just conquered the remaining part of Burma, and the Royal Navy was unchallenged, except for the occasional slave trader off the coast of Africa. The army that lined the route of the Jubilee procession and marched past the Queen at Aldershot was beginning to change from the army that had fought on so many fronts during the Queen's long reign. Better barracks were being built, pay was increased a little and the purchase of commissions was abolished. The First Boer War of 1880 was the last time that the regimental colours were carried into action: thereafter the colours were ceremonially laid up until the regiment returned from war. The Sudan Expedition of 1884 was the last time that the famous red coat of the British Army was seen in action; after that it was only worn on ceremonial occasions. In 1880, a soldier's active life was seven years with the colours and eight for India and the Colonies. The minimum age for enlistment was eighteen, and no man was allowed to go to India before he was twenty. New brooms in the persons of Lord Wolseley and Lord Kitchener did what they could to bring the British Army up to modern standards. Fight well and win they did, often against fearful odds, but they had not fought a European power for fifty years, and severe lessons were to be learned in the Boer War at the end of Victoria's reign before the army regained its laurels.

Transport

Unless you were rich enough to have your own carriage, Londoners travelled by horse-drawn buses. Since they first appeared in 1829, the brightly-coloured buses had sprung up everywhere. Until 1850, the London bus was a single-decker, but then, in defiance of the law that limited the number of passengers a bus could carry, the companies fitted seats on the roof, knife-board fashion, with the passengers sitting back to back. This was the bus to be seen on the streets at the time of the Jubilee, and you knew your bus by its colour, not by the number. The buses had two horses, and the driver sat up on the top deck. He saluted other passing drivers with his whip, and guided his horses skilfully through the chaotic London traffic. Neither he nor the conductor wore uniforms, just bowler hats at a jaunty angle, and maybe pearl buttons on their coats. It was the custom once a year for Lord Rothschild to send a brace of pheasants to every bus driver and conductor in London. To celebrate the event, the drivers tied a bunch of yellow and blue ribbons to their whips – the racing colours of the Rothschilds.

The other means of transport was a cab, and the most famous and typical of the Victorian era was the hansom cab, introduced to London streets in the 1850s. It was called the Gondola of London, as the most romantic form of transport. It was smart, speedy and by no means expensive. The black coachwork shone, the wheels were often painted yellow, and most cabs sported a little vase of flowers inside. All drivers took a pride in their hansoms, and dressed accordingly. An alternative for the elderly or more cautious was the four-wheeler cab, able to carry plenty of luggage, and indeed to accommodate the large Victorian families.

The people of the provinces came up to London by railway, and the companies had laid on special excursion trains from all over the country. These ran from seven o'clock in the morning until one thirty the next morning. The demand was overwhelming, but the various companies managed to cope with thousands of travellers on that special day.

There were three classes of railway carriage, first, second and third, of varying degrees of comfort. Third-class carriages had no upholstery at all, only wooden seats. Those of the second class had upholstered seats, in rows of five abreast. The first-class compartments were sumptuous. Pullman carriages had been introduced in the early 1870s on the Midland Railway and in 1881 the introduction of electric lighting made them the most luxurious way of travelling. In 1879 the first British dining car made its appearance. Until then passengers had had to carry their own refreshment in hampers, which could be ordered at the station. They might contain cold chicken or meat, lettuce, rolls, cheese, fruit, condiments, butter and a small bottle of red wine, complete with knives, forks, spoons and even linen serviettes – all for half-a-crown. On the long distance trains the lack of corridors made journeys uncomfortable, if there were not many stops. Corridor trains were not common until the 1890s and there was a rush at every stop to answer the call of nature. Many travelled from Scotland for the Jubilee, and were able to use the sleeping cars introduced by the North British Railway in 1873, and reasonably common by 1887 on long distance journeys. The popular version was the American Pullman Saloon layout with curtains, offering a degree of privacy. These sleepers required the passenger to undress on the bed – a complicated manoeuvre for Victorian ladies with corsets and bustled skirts. At first the dining cars were the preserve of the first-class passengers, and they were sumptuous indeed. A contemporary description of the Midland Railway Dining Car speaks of 'The interior fittings of richly coloured and figured mahogany, the seats are upholstered with figured crimson or blue moquette, and shaped so as to give the passenger not only a convenient seat while dining, but facility for a comfortable nap after dinner. The two dining cars are connected by the kitchen carriage of adequate size to provide for the dining of 15 first class and 47 third class passengers. This kitchen is fitted up with all the modern appliances for the preserving and well cooking of every kind of food that might be required, and attached thereto are a conductor's pantry and stores.'

Once in London, the excursion passenger could reach the Jubilee route by underground railway, if they had arrived at the Great Western Railway's station at Paddington. The Underground had been opened in 1863, and ran between Paddington and the City of London. At that time the trains were steam, not electric, and the noise was deafening as the train belched its way through clouds of smoke and steam into the station. The passengers breathed a mixture of soot, smoke, and sulphur – not the best way to travel on that hot June day in 1887, in your best Sunday clothes.

Fashions of 1887

Fashions for men in that Jubilee summer were not very different from previous years. The classic male garment for the upper classes was the frock coat. It was the outward sign of stability and respectability for every man of standing from the Prince of Wales downwards, including bank managers, stockbrokers, doctors, actors, and even floorwalkers in the prestigious shops of the West End. It suited all men, stout or slim, and was usually made of black cloth of various qualities, single or double-breasted according to taste. It was cut high or low with black silk lapels. Grey was another popular colour, especially in summer. The waistcoat could be black, white, or spotted; made of figured silk or the same material as the suit. Coloured waistcoats smacked of the theatre or the fast set and were thought to be not quite the thing. Across the chest hung a heavy gold chain, and at one end a gold watch – a hunter, half hunter, or a repeater. At the other end was a gold sovereign purse. In the centre of the chain was usually a seal. Shirts were made of white linen with starched fronts and round starched cuffs. The collar was also starched, with a black silk tie or a spotted four-in-hand fastened with a gold tie-pin, often shaped as a horse's head or a fox, a hunting horn or occasionally a lady's leg. Trousers were of the pepper-and-salt pattern or striped; plain grey was often worn with a grey frock coat. Boots were always black, made of kid or patent leather. Men always wore gloves and a hat. With a frock coat this would be a top hat, bound in silk and with a high gloss. The hat band was of black cloth. Younger men preferred the morning coat, cut away to show a waistcoat of contrasting colour, but again always worn with a top hat. Lower down the social scale a dark suit was the dress for all occasions, in various qualities of cloth, but always with a hat, usually the bowler, common to all walks of life as can be seen in the photographs. Straw hats were popular for the country or seaside, but not often seen in the city. Men's underclothing changed little throughout the period; made of wool of an uncomfortable texture, with high necks and long sleeves, but born with typical Victorian grit.

The ladies sitting in the stands and boxes along the Jubilee route would be decked in the latest fashion, which was always changing, unlike the men's clothes. There were perpetual variations in style and material. Pure silks and satins, lawn and muslin were produced in colours as exotic as their names; tan dor, raisin d'espagne, garnet, and ottoman. All the clothes were made by hand in the workshops of the couturiers, who remained the real arbiters of fashion. 'No two women are dressed the same', wrote one observer. There were sometimes over thirty different materials available in one year. In 1885 there was a slight revival of the bustle, but this did not last. The two-piece dress was growing more popular, as the fore-runner of the tailor-made suit, which became indispensable for a lady's wardrobe. Stockings were of silk and usually chosen to match the dress. In the street ladies almost always wore buttoned or half-laced boots, usually made of leather instead of cloth as had been customary. Hats were indispensable, large or small, decorated with feathers and even birds themselves. On hot summer days ladies carried parasols to protect themselves from the sun, as it was fashionable to be pale, not tanned brown by the sun. Indeed, veils were often worn in summer. The women of lower-classes wore ready-made clothes from the large department stores, and the invention of the sewing machine had also given a boost to home dressmaking. A huge influx of cheap ready-made clothes in cotton or fustian had come from the Continent. In summer a white blouse and skirt was the ideal costume: it accentuated the fashionable narrow waist-line, which was often only 22 inches and sometimes less, but as always in the interests of fashion the ladies suffered in silence until the next season, or whenever the style would change.

The Police of 1887

The police force that controlled the crowds at the Jubilee had been formed in 1829, some ten years after Queen Victoria's birth. They had gradually won the confidence and trust of the general public and were now held in great esteem. There were about 12,000 policemen in London in 1887. The police headquarters was at Scotland Yard near Whitehall Palace. By the 1860s the country boasted an efficient police force.

The last public execution in London was in 1868 at Clerkenwell when the Fenian Daniel Barrett was hanged for a bomb outrage. The treadmill lasted until 1898, but flogging continued well after this. At the end of 1887 there was a huge demonstration against unemployment in Trafalgar Square. It was dispersed by the police and the Life Guards after the reading of the Riot Act. Ten people were killed and more than one hundred were injured. The Special Branch were formed in the 1860s to combat a series of bomb attacks by Fenians in London. There were attacks on the Underground between Charing Cross and Westminster and at Paddington, where nearly seventy people were injured in 1883. Government offices in King Charles Street and *The Times* offices were bombed, and in 1884 Scotland Yard was so badly damaged by a bomb that a new building was required. This was built by convicts near the Houses of Parliament and opened the year after the Jubilee in 1888. It was called New Scotland Yard. The London constables were paid twenty-four shillings per week with a pension to look forward to. The uniform worn at the time of the Jubilee was to last for the next fifty years. The helmet with a badge was introduced in 1865, and the single-breasted tunic with a two-inch high collar at about the same time. The truncheon in its own leather case was attached to the leather belt, but in 1881 it was carried in a special pocket in the trousers, as is customary to this day. At night the dark lantern was also attached to the belt. This was so called because it could be revolved by turning the top to shine a light when required. The police whistle was introduced in 1884, as the police had found the old-fashioned rattle cumbersome and out-of-date. The whistle was handier and could be heard over the noise of London's traffic at a distance of some 900 yards.

London's Entertainments

May of the Jubilee year was marked by the arrival of the Wild West Circus of Buffalo Bill Cody. The cast of two hundred included Indians, cowboys and Mexicans. There were also horses, buffaloes, Texas steers, burros, broncos, a stage-coach, wagons and tents, not to mention several bands. A vast crowd watched with mounting excitement as their ship docked at the Royal Albert Dock in East London. A train was provided to take all the passengers and animals to the Earl's Court grounds in Kensington. The showground was already prepared and an open grandstand held 10,000 people. Sheltered stands held 10,000 more, and there was standing room for another 10,000. The show was of course a rousing success. The Queen herself visited the grounds intending to stop for only an hour, but remained for the whole performance. All society flocked to the show; the Prince and Princess of Wales, Grand Duke Michael of Russia, the Duke of Cambridge, the Duke of Teck, the Comtesse de Paris, politicans, actors and actresses. Queen Victoria was so impressed that she insisted on seeing the show again, and arranged for a performance at Windsor Castle on the day before the Jubilee. It was on this occasion that four kings rode in the deadwood stage-coach; the King of Greece, the King of Saxony, the King of Belgium and the King of Denmark. The Prince of Wales rode on the box. The Prince remarked to Buffalo Bill that he held a good poker hand – four kings. Buffalo Bill replied, not only four kings, but a Prince as well, which made it a royal flush such as no man had ever held before. He later told his friends that story and added, 'not only that but I held the Royal Joker as well'. The triumphant Wild West Company returned to New York in the spring of 1888, having earned Buffalo Bill a small fortune.

As light relief after the Jubilee celebrations, a visit to the theatre was a good way to round off the day in London. Evening dress was essential to sit in the stalls or boxes, and indeed nobody would think of presenting themselves for admission to the more august seats unless they were dressed for the occasion. Dress was not so particular in the upper circle where seats cost four shillings and could be reserved. A seat in the pit cost two-and-sixpence, and in the gallery a shilling. Programmes were often free, as was the cloakroom. Theatres closed in August and September to prepare for a new season's production, and also because London society was out of town at this time. Besides the theatres there were the music halls, which had at this time a slightly risqué reputation. Drinking was allowed and ladies did not venture here until the turn of the century when the licences were revoked. The music halls were the stronghold of such famous artistes as Marie Lloyd, Dan Leno and Lottie Collins, famous for her abandoned dancing. This was often the haunt of women, not ladies, but gradually the music halls changed their ways and became more suitable for a mixed audience. By the 1880s there were over 270 variety theatres in London, not counting the legitimate theatre.

The people worked hard and for long hours. Holidays were few, and Bank Holidays had only been introduced in 1871. The year 1886 had seen the introduction of the Shop Hours Act, which restricted the employment of people under the age of eighteen to a seventy-hour week. That would mean a thirteen-and-a-half-hour day with a Saturday of six and a half hours. So the Jubilee holiday was indeed a special occasion for the British people and a triumph for the English crown. People came from far and wide to celebrate this day with their Queen, and not even her wedding or that of the Prince of Wales had been accorded such love and enthusiasm as that shown on this Jubilee day.

PERSONALITIES AT THE JUBILEE

2
Queen Victoria, 1887

This was the Queen's official portrait for the Jubilee. Her Majesty was
dressed in black, as was her custom since the death of Prince Albert, albeit
black figured silk, relieved by a white Spanish lace bonnet ornamented
with diamonds. The Queen also wore the stars of her two favourite orders:
the Most Noble Order of the Garter and the Most Exalted Order of the
Star of India. Queen Victoria was a striking figure, dressed in black amidst
her brilliant court.

3 Left
Edward and Alexandra, Prince and Princess of Wales, 1887

Prince Edward was the eldest son and heir of Queen Victoria. Born in 1841, he was forty-five at the time of the Jubilee. In 1863 he married Princess Alexandra, the eldest daughter of King Christian IX of Denmark. She was a great beauty of her day, as were her two sisters; Princess Dagmar who married the Emperor Alexander III of All The Russias, and Princess Thyra who married the Crown Prince of Hanover. The Prince and Princess of Wales had six children, three boys and three girls.

4
Albert Victor, Duke of Clarence and Avondale, 1887

Prince Albert Victor was the eldest son of Edward, Prince of Wales, and in direct line of succession to the throne of Great Britain after his father. At the time of the Jubilee the prince was twenty-three years old. He was to fall in love several times with beautiful young women, including his cousin the dazzling Princess Alix of Hesse and By Rhine, Lady Sybil St Clair Erskine, and Princess Hélène of Orleans, daughter of the Pretender to the throne of France. To the relief of his parents and Queen Victoria, he became engaged to Princess Mary of Teck in 1891. However, the Prince died of pneumonia the following year, before the marriage could take place.

5 Left
Prince George of Wales

Prince George was the younger son of Edward, Prince of Wales. He became heir to the throne in 1892 when his elder brother died of pneumonia. At the time of the Jubilee he was pursuing a career in the Royal Navy. He had qualified as a Lieutenant in 1885 and served on HMS *Thunderer* and HMS *Alexandra.* The Prince hoped to marry his cousin Princess Marie, daughter of Alfred, Duke of Edinburgh. However, she rejected his suit and became engaged to the Crown Prince of Roumania. The Prince recovered from the blow and eventually married his late brother's intended bride, Princess Mary of Teck.

6 Right
Prince George, Duke of Cambridge, Earl of Tipperary

Prince George was a grandson of King George III. A bluff hearty character, he was blundering, and sometimes a little too much like his Hanoverian uncles for Queen Victoria's taste. However, he held a special place in the Queen's regard as her cousin and close relative. He was created a Knight of the Garter in 1835 and became a field marshal in the Army in 1862. At the time of the Jubilee he was Commander-in-Chief of the British Army. He is wearing the uniform of the Grenadier Guards, of which he was Colonel.

7 Left
John Campbell, Marquis of Lorne

The Marquis married Queen
Victoria's daughter Louise in 1871.
He was Governor-General of
Canada from 1878 to 1883. It was
at this time that the Princess
suffered an appalling accident,
when she fell from a sledge, was
dragged by her hair for some
distance and lost her ear. The
Marquis eventually succeeded his
father as Duke of Argyll, and died
in 1914.

8 Right
Crown Prince Friedrich of Prussia

The favourite son-in-law of Queen
Victoria and husband of her eldest
daughter, Victoria, Princess Royal.
He was the son and heir of the first
Emperor of Germany, King
Wilhelm of Prussia. He was to
succeed as Emperor in 1888, but he
was then already dying of throat
cancer, and reigned for only three
months. A tall and powerfully built
man, he caused delighted comment
amongst the crowd at the Jubilee
procession, mounted on a heavy
charger, and wearing a Prussian
uniform, steel cuirass and helmet
surmounted by a silver imperial
eagle.

9 Left
Victoria, Crown Princess of Prussia

Princess Victoria was the eldest child of Queen Victoria and Prince Albert. She was born in 1840 and betrothed at the age of fifteen to Prince Friedrich Wilhelm of Prussia. They were married in 1858 at the Chapel Royal, St James' Palace. The royal couple had eight children, four boys and four girls. The eldest was born by breech birth and his arm was permanantly damaged. He was to be the future Emperor Wilhelm II. Victoria's sick husband eventually succeeded as Emperor of Germany, but only reigned for ninety days. The Empress Victoria died of cancer of the spine in August 1901.

10
Wilhelm, Prince of Prussia, 1887

Prince Wilhelm was the eldest son of Crown Prince Friedrich of Prussia and Princess Victoria of England. There was a great affection between him and Queen Victoria, as he was her first grandson. In 1881 the Prince married Princess Auguste, daughter of Duke Friedrich of Schleswig-Holstein-Sonderburg-Augustenburg. His father and grandfather were both to die in 1888, when he succeeded as Emperor of Germany and King of Prussia.

12 Right
*King Christian IX and
Queen Louise of Denmark, 1887*

In his youth King Christian IX had been considered as a husband for Queen Victoria, but in 1863 he had succeeded his kinsman Frederik VII as King of Denmark. Queen Louise was the daughter of Wilhelm, Landgrave of Hesse Cassel. Their daughter, Princess Alexandra, was married to Edward, Prince of Wales.

11
Albert I, King of Saxony, 1887

The King had succeeded his father Johann I in 1873. He had been invited to the Jubilee as a personal friend of Queen Victoria and, perhaps more importantly, as a friend of the late Prince Albert. The King had distinguished himself as a general in the Franco-Prussian War of 1870, and had been made a field marshal of the Prussian Army. His wife, Queen Carola, was the last direct descendant of the Swedish Royal House of Vasa.

13 Opposite
King George I and Queen Olga of Greece

Prince Wilhelm of Denmark had adopted the name George in 1863 when
he was elected King of Greece at the age of only eighteen. He married
Grand Duchess Olga of Russia in 1867, when she was only sixteen. Their
fourth son, Prince Andrew of Greece, was the father of Prince Philip,
Duke of Edinburgh.

14
Leopold II, King of the Belgians

The king spent many of his later years on the French Riviera where he had
a villa. He had become immensely rich by his development of the Congo
Free State in Central Africa. He was unhappily married to Grand Duchess
Marie of Austria, and his second daughter Stephanie was married to the
ill-fated Crown Prince Rudolph of Austria. His son Prince Leopold, Duke
of Brabant had died in 1869.

15 Left
Crown Prince Rudolph of Austria

The Crown Prince was twenty-nine when he came to London for the Jubilee. He had been married for six years to Princess Stephanie of Belgium, and they had a four-year-old daughter, Princess Elisabeth Marie. In 1889 the Crown Prince committed suicide with his mistress, Countess Maria Vetsera.

16
Crown Prince Carlos of Portugal

The Crown Prince was a great friend of the Prince of Wales. He was a womaniser, a man of the world, and an excellent shot. He was also a painter of some talent. In 1886 he married Princess Amélie of Orleans, the beautiful daughter of the Count of Paris, head of the Royal House of France. They had one child at this time, the four-month-old Prince Luis Filipe.

17
Crown Prince Gustav of Sweden

The Crown Prince was married to Princess Viktoria of Baden and they had two young sons at the time of the Jubilee; Prince Oscar and Prince Wilhelm. The eldest son was to marry Princess Margaret, daughter of Prince Arthur, Duke of Connaught and Strathearn. The Crown Prince was twenty-nine in 1887 and succeeded his father King Oscar II in 1907.

18 Right
Amadeo Ferdinando, Duke of Aosta

Prince Amadeo was the second son of King Vittorio Emanuele II of Italy. When Queen Isabella of Spain and the Indies had been deposed in 1868, the throne was offered to him. He was married to Princess Maria Vittoria of Cisterna e di Belriguardo and they had nine children. Their grandson Amadeo, Duke of Aosta, was Governor General of Italian East Africa during the Second World War.

20 Right
Prince Edward of Saxe-Weimar-Eisenach

Prince Edward was the son of Prince Bernhard of Saxe-Weimar-Eisenach. He settled in England and made the British Army his career, becoming Colonel of the First Life Guards and a general of the Army. He married Lady Augusta Gordon Lennox, daughter of the Duke of Richmond. The Prince had been wounded in action in the Crimean War in 1855.

19
Grand Duke Sergei and Grand Duchess Elisabeth of Russia, 1887

The Grand Duke was the fifth son of Emperor Alexander II of All The Russias. He was born in 1857 and married Princess Elisabeth of Hesse and By Rhine in 1884. His elder brother, Alexander III, had succeeded as Emperor in 1881. An unpopular Governor of Moscow, the Grand Duke was killed by an anarchist's bomb in 1904, while driving out of the Kremlin.

22 Right
The Duke and Duchess of Teck and their two eldest children, 1887

The father of Duke Franz of Teck had been heir to the throne of Württemburg, but forfeited his rights when he married Countess Claudine von Rhedey de Kis Rhede. Duke Franz married Mary Adelaide, the daughter of Prince Adolphus, Duke of Cambridge. The Duchess was very stout, but a friendly, lively woman who was popular with the people. The Tecks were always in debt, despite an income of £8,000 a year, as they were spending around £15,000 a year. Their debts were eventually cleared and they retired to Florence, but returned at the invitation of Queen Victoria to live at White Lodge in Richmond Park. Princess Mary became engaged to Prince Albert Victor, Duke of Clarence and Avondale in 1891. Prince Adolphus married Lady Margaret Grosvenor, daughter of the Duke of Westminster, in 1894.

21
Baron and Baroness von Pawel Rammingen, 1887

The Baroness was the former Princess Frederike of Hanover, daughter of King Georg V who had lost his throne to Prussia after the disastrous war of 1866. Baron Alfons von Pawel Rammingen's family came from Coburg and the couple were married in the private chapel of Windsor Castle in 1880. The Baroness was a great-grand-daughter of George III.

23
The Maharajah of Gondal

The Maharajah ruled a Rajput Hindu state of about one thousand square miles in the Western Indian States Agency. He was only twenty-two at the time of the Jubilee celebrations. He had studied medicine at Edinburgh and qualified as a doctor, and was also one of the first Indian Princes to be selected for the honour of a Knight Commander of the Order of the British Empire.

24 Opposite
The Maharajah of Morvi

Born in 1858 the Prince was a Rajput Hindu ruling a small state of only 800 square miles in the Western Indian Agency. He maintained a large racing stable and entered his horses at the Bombay Meetings during the cool season. He also enjoyed a large revenue from this very populous state.

25 Left
Horse and trappings presented by an Indian prince, 1887

On the celebration of her Jubilee, Queen Victoria received many gifts from her subjects and the Empire. His Highness the Thakor of Morvi gave the Queen a magnificent Arab stallion complete with costly saddlery and trappings made of gold and silver.

26
The Thakor Sahib of Limbdi

A Rajput Hindu Prince ruling a small state of only three hundred square miles in the Western Indian Agency. This was in the Kathiawar Peninsula where two hundred and eighty-two princes ruled an area about the size of Ireland between them.

28 Right
The Maharajah Holkar of Indore

The Maharajah had succeeded to the throne in the year before the Jubilee. Indore was one of the larger Indian states of some ten thousand square miles and the Prince enjoyed an income of about one million pounds sterling per year – and that was at the rate of 1887. The state was formed in 1725 when the Mogul Empire declined and the Holkars carved out their own states in Central India.

27
The Maharao of Cutch

This Prince's ancestors had migrated from the Scinde in north-west India to conquer this country in 1549. It consisted of 7,000 square miles to the north of Bombay and was a very rich state due to its position on the coast, which encouraged prolific trade with East Africa and Arabia. The Maharao had succeeded to the throne when he was ten years old and was twenty-one at the time of the Jubilee. His younger brother accompanied him to London for the celebrations.

29 Left
The Maharani of Cooch Bihar, 1887

The Maharani accompanied her husband to the Jubilee and was received by Queen Victoria at Windsor Castle. It was unusual for the wife of the ruler to be seen out of purdah, but the state of Cooch Bihar was well known among the princely states of India for its emancipated outlook.

30 Right
The Maharajah of Cooch Bihar, 1887

This Indian state lay to the north of Bengal and covered some 1,000 square miles of territory. It was a Hindu state and came under British influence in 1772, after they had come to the Maharajah's aid against Bhutan. This was a popular country for sportsmen due to the large supply of game, particularly tigers, to be found in the jungle areas.

Princess Liliuokalani of Hawaii, 1887

The Princess accompanied her mother on their tour of Europe, and was also present at the Jubilee. She later succeeded as Queen of Hawaii, and her stubborn resistance to the planters, missionaries, and traders led to an American-inspired revolution in 1893. The United States Minister ordered a party of marines ashore to protect the Americans although none appeared to be obviously threatened. The islands were annexed in 1898 by the United States of America.

31
Queen Kapiolani of Hawaii, 1887

The Queen was on a visit to Europe and was invited by Queen Victoria to the Jubilee celebrations. Queen Kapiolani was the wife of King Kalakaua of Hawaii, who had in the year of the Jubilee leased to the United States of America a naval base known as Pearl Harbour.

33
Queen Kapiolani of Hawaii and her daughter Princess Liliuokalani at the home of Colonel Stewart, 1887

When the Queen and her party visited England for the Jubilee, they were invited by Colonel and Mrs Stewart to stay at their country seat in Norfolk. The Queen is seated in the centre with her daughter. Mrs Stewart is on her right.

THE JUBILEE PROCESSION

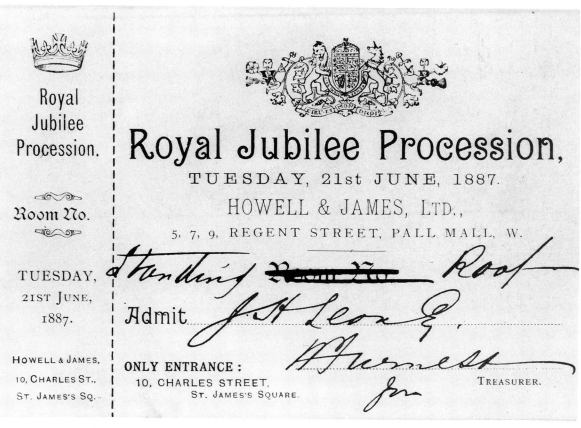

34
Royal Jubilee ticket

This ticket for seats to view the procession was issued by Howell and James Ltd, who had premises in Regent Street, Pall Mall. Evidently the demand was so great that they sold space on the roof as well.

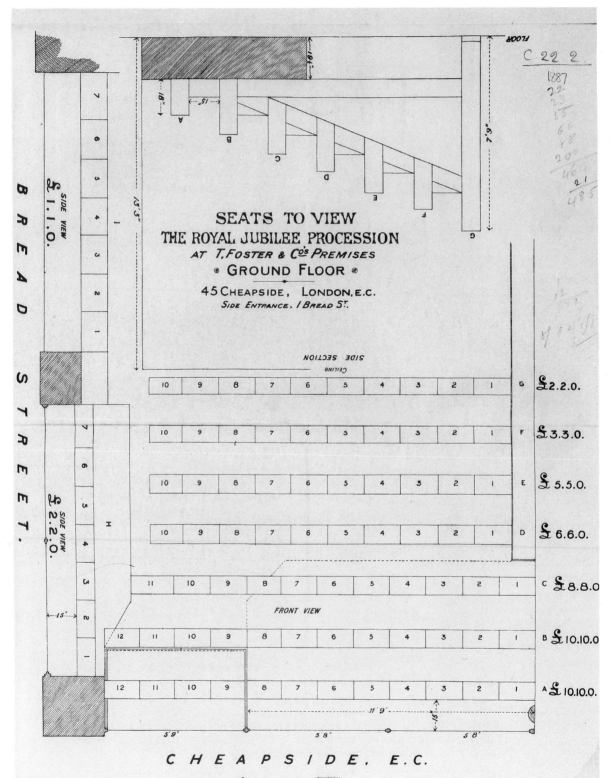

SEATS TO VIEW
THE ROYAL JUBILEE PROCESSION
AT *T. FOSTER & C^{os} PREMISES*
⦿ GROUND FLOOR ⦿

45 CHEAPSIDE, LONDON, E.C.
SIDE ENTRANCE, 1 BREAD ST.

35 Left
Seating plan to view the procession

Shops and businesses with premises along the route of the procession lost no time in erecting stands and selling space. At Foster and Co., seats cost from one guinea up to ten guineas for the best seats, facing Cheapside in the City.

36
Erecting stands for the Jubilee, 1887

This was in the days before metal tubular scaffolding, so everything was made of solid wood, as can be seen in the preparations for the great day. These were official stands near the Abbey and were not sold commercially.

37
Buildings erected outside the Abbey, 1887

Outside Westminster Abbey, wooden buildings were erected to
accommodate the officials and to receive important guests from their
carriages, before they proceeded into the Abbey itself. To the upper left
can be seen seating stands with flagstaff decorations.

38
Indian princes crossing Westminster Bridge

On the right can be seen the stands erected within the Houses of
Parliament for the members and their guests. Foot guards are lining the
route, and drawn up across Whitehall on the left is a troop of Life Guards.
Opposite is a squadron of Dragoon Guards.

39 Left
*The Duke and Duchess of Teck
entering Waterloo Place*

The Duchess of Teck was a
particular favourite of the people of
London. Although travelling in a
closed carriage, whenever she leant
out of the window she was sure to
receive a rousing cheer from the
crowds. A troop of Life Guards
precede and follow the coach.
Some of the elaborate street
decorations built across Lower
Regent Street can also be seen.

40
The procession passing through Parliament Square

These are the closed carriages of the important guests of the Queen, and
the Grenadier Guards lining the route have been brought up to the present
arms position. On the right are some of the stands erected for Members of
Parliament and their guests. On the lower right on the pavement, watching
the arrivals, can be seen a number of footmen, recognisable by their
buttoned coats, stockings and hats trimmed with gold lace.

41
The Queen's carriage preceded by the Indian Escort

As several Indian Princes were invited to the Jubilee celebrations, it was decided to include representatives of the Indian Cavalry in the procession. The escort was under the comand of Captain Charles W. Muir who had served as Commandant of the Governor-General's bodyguard since 1885. Before returning to India each member of the escort was presented with a Jubilee medal by Her Majesty in a ceremony at Windsor Castle.

42
The Queen's carriage passing through Waterloo Place

Queen Victoria sits in the back of the carriage looking forward. Facing her is Princess Alexandra of Wales, with the white parasol. Queen Victoria's eldest daughter, Crown Princess Victoria of Prussia, is sitting next to the Queen. The columned building on the left is Rivingtons the Booksellers.

43
Carriages of the Indian princes

The Londoners gave a rousing cheer for the brilliantly dressed Indian princes, particularly the Maharao of Cutch, whose diamond-and-ruby-encrusted turban flashed and sparkled in the bright sunshine. The Grenadier Guards are lining this part of the route, and two pioneer sergeants with their axes can be seen in the foreground.

44
Queen Victoria arrives at Westminster Abbey

The grooms are holding the heads of the Queen's Hanoverian horses, as the royal party alight. Drawn up outside is a guard of honour from the Royal Navy. They are wearing their summer rig, including the distinctive sennet hat, very cool and sensible on that hot summer's day.

45
Royal guests arriving at Westminster Abbey

On the left of centre on horseback is Prince George, Duke of Cambridge, Commander-in-Chief of the British Army and a cousin of the Queen. In the foreground are the foreign princes who rode in the procession. The grooms are collecting the horses so that the guests may proceed into the Abbey. There does not appear to be the co-ordination and precision to which we have grown accustomed in royal functions in modern times.

46
Waiting for the Queen at the Abbey

During the ceremony the carriages were assembled at Broad Sanctuary to await the Queen and other guests. In the foreground can be seen Life Guard Officers and staff officers in their cocked hats. In the centre is an officer of the Indian Army talking to a Life Guard. To the right is the Queen's carriage with its distinctive Hanoverian greys: her thoughtful coachmen have closed up the carriage to try and keep the leather interior cool, away from the hot sun. In the background are the Life Guards, drawn up at ease. Behind them is St Stephen's Hall, offering a Jubilee lunch.

CELEBRATIONS
IN LONDON AND
THE COUNTRY

47
Slough railway station, awaiting the arrival of Queen Victoria

This was the day after the celebrations in London, when the Queen
returned to Windsor Castle to rest. In the foreground are drawn up a
squadron of the Royal Horse Guards who were stationed at Combermere
Barracks. The cavalry escort includes a state trumpeter on the extreme
right. In the background is the British Orphan Asylum which was originally
built as the Royal Hotel for the Great Western Railway Company.

48 Left
Programme for the Lord Mayor of London's Ball and Reception

This was held at the Guildhall on 28 June by the Lord Mayor, Sir Reginald Hanson, to celebrate the Jubilee. The Prince and Princess of Wales were present together with a large number of foreign princes and distinguished guests from all over the Empire.

49
The royal tent at Queen Victoria's garden party, 1887

The Queen held a garden party at Buckingham Palace on 29 June 1887. A tent was erected in the grounds so that the Queen could rest. It was guarded by members of her Indian escort. The nearest officer is the senior native officer of the Viceroy's bodyguard, Subadar Sheik Imdad Ali. His uniform is scarlet with gold embroidery. The next officer is Risaldar Major Nural Hussun of the 6th Prince of Wales Bengal Cavalry. His uniform is blue with red facings and gold lace.

50
Queen Victoria's garden party, 1887

View across the lake with the guests on the far side. The Jubilee Garden
Party was a special occasion with many distinguished guests from all over
the Empire. Mr Gladstone was invited, but Queen Victoria successfully
managed to avoid him all day.

51
Queen Victoria at the Army Review, Aldershot, 9 July 1887

The Queen's carriage is the first in the line on the left, drawn by her Hanoverian greys. On horseback next to the royal coach is the Commander-in-Chief Prince George, Duke of Cambridge. Queen Victoria was reviewing the regular and auxiliary forces, and the troops about to pass the Queen are the London Scottish in their distinctive grey kilted uniforms.

52
Queen Victoria's Indian Escort at Windsor Castle, 1887

It was decided that the Indian Army would provide Her Majesty with a personal escort in the Jubilee procession. On the extreme right stands the commandant of the Viceroy's bodyguard, who was in command of the escort, Captain Charles W. Muir. At the other end of the group stands the only other British officer, Captain G.A. Money of the 18th Bengal Lancers. Standing next to him is a fine old Sikh officer and veteran of the Indian Mutiny, Risaldar Major Sher Singh, of the 2nd Punjab Cavalry. The bemedalled officer fifth from the left is Risaldar Major Ishree Singh of the 19th Bengal Lancers, who fought not only in the Indian Mutiny but also in China in 1860 and in Afghanistan in 1878/80.

SPITHEAD, JULY 23RD, 1887.

FATHER NEPTUNE (*cheerily*). "WHAT—VULCAN, MY HEARTY! WELL, WE'RE SHIPMATES NOW, SO HERE'S 'THE QUEEN!'—GOD BLESS HER!!"

53
Spithead, 23 July 1887

Great Britain displayed her might as a sea power before the Queen and her guests at the Great Review at Spithead. Over a hundred warships and twenty thousand sailors took part. The cartoon emphasises the change in ships from the days of wooden walls to modern iron-clad warships.

54
On the deck of the Royal Yacht, Spithead 1887

The Royal Naval Review at Spithead, 23 July 1887. A view of the deck of
the Royal Yacht *Victoria and Albert*, with the crew in the special rig worn on
the Royal Yacht. The summer rig consisted of a white V-necked frock with
decorative blue cuffs and a broad blue collar edged with three white lines.
The frock was loosely tucked into bell-bottomed trousers. Sennet hats
were also worn.

55
The Review of the Fleet at Spithead, 1887

The Royal Yacht *Victoria and Albert* has just passed one of the battle cruisers which is dressed overall. The sailors can be seen standing on the masts and rigging. Although this is a steamship, sails were also carried – common practice for many years on ships of the Royal Navy.

56
The Braemar Gathering, 1 September 1887

Queen Victoria is seated in the royal pavilion in the centre. After the rigours of the Jubilee celebrations, the Queen was glad to retire to her beloved Highlands. By her own command the Highland gathering was held at Balmoral.

57
Jubilee celebrations at Basingstoke, 1887

At the market place in Basingstoke, Hampshire, grace is being said before sitting down to the Jubilee lunch. The umbrellas show how hot it was on the great day. In the centre stands a photographer with his tripod camera, taking pictures of the town worthies.

58
Jubilee lunch at North Walsham, 1887

The tables are spread right down the High Street of this North Norfolk
town. The street appears to be very crowded and every table place is
occupied. No doubt lunch was served at one o'clock, as the clock in the
photograph stands at one twenty.

59
Jubilee lunch for the old people, 1887

Here at Sutton Coldfield the celebrations for the Queen's Jubilee included a lunch for the old and poor of the town. It was held in a marquee erected next to the Town Hall. No doubt some of these people were the same age as the Queen. There was of course no retirement age nor pension in those days, so people carried on working well into old age.

60
Jubilee procession, Sutton Coldfield, 1887

A procession of carriages of all types is followed by the town band, then the trade unionists with their large banner. The procession is heading for the park for the Jubilee celebration. On the left can be seen a gentleman riding a large tricycle.

61
Jubilee lunch at Hertford, 1887

Many charitable organisations gave a luncheon to the poor to celebrate the
Queen's Jubilee. At Hertford it was held in the Corn Exchange. At the
back of the hall are the carvers in their white aprons, while the ladies and
gentlemen serve the roast beef.

62
Procession of school children at Oxford, 1887

7,000 school children marched down Broad Street on 28 June, a week later than Jubilee Day, so as not to interrupt Commemoration Week. The procession took 45 minutes to pass by. In the University Parks the Corporation entertained the children to tea. They consumed 22 cwt of cake, 130 gallons of milk, 86 lb of tea and 5 cwt of sugar.

63
Roasting an ox at Osney, Oxford, 1887

In many parts of the kingdom, it was traditional to roast an ox as part of any major celebration. At Osney the cost was met by public subscription and the meat was given away free with some bread. Some of the men are wearing favours in their buttonholes, bearing the Queen's portrait and the Jubilee date.

64
*West Street, Horsham, 21 June
1887*

All the small towns and villages
celebrated the Jubilee and
decorated the streets with flags and
bunting. The schools were closed
and the day declared a public
holiday.

65 Right
Basingstoke Town Hall, 1887

The Town Hall is decorated for the Jubilee celebration. The clock tower
was added at this time. The façade is adorned with portraits of the Queen
as a young girl of eighteen and as the well-loved and respected old lady of
her Jubilee year. Under the centre awning is a bust of the Queen,
surrounded by members of the town council.

66
Triumphal Arch, Kensington High Street, 1887

Arches of this kind were a common form of decoration in the Victorian age. They would be very solidly made of wood and canvas, and a great deal of hard work would go into their construction. In the centre can be seen a road sweeper – a very important person in the days of horse-drawn traffic.

LONDON AND LONDON CHARACTERS OF THE 1880s

67
Shop decoration, Kensington, 1887

The Shop of Wells and Co, Jewellers By Appointment to Her Majesty, is decorated in a tasteful manner suitable to such a prestigious shop. The Queen's initials are spelled out in electric lights and there is also a sunburst effect above. Next door, the florist has not quite managed the flamboyance of his neighbour, but the 'Duke of Cumberland' public house has a brave flower display.

68 Left
Shop Decoration, Kensington, 1887

Another fashionable shop in this prestigious area has been decorated for the Queen's Jubilee. Herbert and Jones, confectioners for weddings, balls and suppers, claimed to be the oldest cooks and confectioners in London. The display consists of coloured lights and a floral tribute above the shop. On the corner can be seen the royal coat of arms, showing that the shop held the Royal Warrant.

69
Kensington High Street, 1887

View looking east by Kensington Gardens. In the background a triumphal arch has been erected across the street. It is a very busy time of day to judge by the amount of traffic on the road. As there are quite a few private carriages it is probably about four in the afternoon, which was the fashionable time for ladies to visit the shops.

70
Looking west from the east end of Kensington High Street, June 1887

The street is decorated with flags of all nations and many of the buildings have their own displays. A large party of gentlemen are outside the King's Arms Hotel, the front of which is decorated with huge lamps, typical of the old gin palaces of the period. Down the street can be seen a theatre covered with electric lights, which will come into its own at dusk.

THE NEW "HATCH."

Mr. P. "AH! THEY'RE AN AWFULLY UGLY LOT! I *DID* THINK THE OLD GAUCHE-HEN—(AHEM!)—WOULD HA' DONE BETTER THAN THAT!!!"

[*Exit sadly.*

71
The New Hatch

The image of the Queen on the new coins struck for the Jubilee failed to please the public from the artistic point of view. Mr Goschen, the new Chancellor of the Exchequer, incurred a great deal of chaff in consequence.

72
Buckingham Palace, 1887

Queen Victoria's London residence was built in 1703 by John Sheffield, Duke of Buckingham. It was purchased by George III, remodelled by George IV, and altered again by Queen Victoria to accommodate her ever-growing young family. She added the east front, seen in the photograph, which overlooks St James's Park. It was completed in 1847 and made Buckingham Palace the ugliest in Europe from the outside. By 1913 the façade had been altered by Sir Aston Webb to the palace we know today. The front was raised to hide the ugly chimneys and roofs, and columns were placed between each window façade.

73 Right
London Bridge, 1887

This was the new bridge built in 1831 to carry the heavy traffic south of the Thames into the City of London. The lamp-posts on the bridge were cast from French cannon captured in the Peninsular Campaign. Until the opening of Tower Bridge in 1894 this was the busiest crossing in London.

74
The Strand, 1887

From early morning until well past midnight the Strand was one of the busiest thoroughfares, containing theatres, shops, law courts and the Inland Revenue. By the time of the Jubilee however, many of the more fashionable shops had moved to the West End – a trend which had begun with the building of Regent Street.

75
Trafalgar Square, 1887

The Jubilee procession passed through this famous square, which has
changed little over the years. On the left is the massive Grand Hotel
erected after the demolition of Northumberland House in 1874, as the
town residence of the Dukes of Northumberland. Straight ahead can be
seen the tower of Big Ben and the Houses of Parliament, nearly a mile away
down Whitehall.

76
Regent Street, 1887

Looking north towards Oxford Street, on the left is Vigo Street and standing on the corner site is the company of Scott Adie, By Appointment to the Queen as can be seen by the royal coat of arms above the door. They sold country clothes and waterproofs, tartan cloth and hosiery, all made in Scotland. Above the door was a large gas bracket in the form of a giant thistle, which burst into a blaze of light at dusk.

77
Regent Street, 1887

Showing the magnificent sweep of the quadrant. Originally there was a
Doric colonnade of cast iron projecting over the pavement on either side.
These were removed in 1848 because they tended to darken the shops.
The balconies were added at this time. In the centre of the street is a cab
rank and many hansom cabs are travelling up and down this fashionable
and expensive shopping area.

78 Left
Tottenham Court Road, 1887

Looking up Tottenham Court Road from Oxford Street and Charing Cross Road. On the right-hand side, the prison-like building is Meux's Brewery, founded in the reign of George III and covering four acres of valuable land. Adjoining the brewery is the Horseshoe Tavern, so-called because of the shape of the dining room. By the 1880s, the modest tavern had grown into a large hotel. On the left an early pattern omnibus without a top deck advertises fares – Oxford Street and Euston Road, all the way for one halfpenny.

79
London slum, 1887

Behind the bright and expensive shops of the Strand ran acres of small alleys and streets. The place was overcrowded and an open drain without sanitation. Gin palaces with their bright gas lamps were the only places to offer something to relieve the monotonous lives of the poor.

80
The London Docks, 1887

The Port of London was busy and thriving in the 1880s. The empire had been built on trade, and by the last quarter of the Victorian era, British traders dominated the world. Here a clipper ship unloads the tribute of the Empire, maybe tea from India, or wool from Australia. The Docks had four gates into the Thames, could hold 300 large vessels, and employed 3,000 men every day.

81
South-Eastern Railway, 1885

Many people travelled by train to get to the Jubilee celebrations. This company, like many others, offered excursions on the great day. The head guard, as seen here, was at the front of the train. He is signalling to the rear guard at the other end. The train is a Richard Mansells Nine Gunboat 0-4-4 Tank Engine, built for suburban line work.

82
Hansom cab, c.1887

An elegant way to travel around the streets of London at Jubilee time. The name above the window shows that this was a company-owned cab. Thomas Tilling had a fleet of buses and cabs which were smartly turned out and always with well-groomed horses. They were by far the quickest way to catch a train or get to an appointment. The fare was one shilling for two miles within a four-mile radius of Charing Cross and double beyond that.

83
Knifeboard bus, 1887

London also had many buses at that time. This bus is standing outside
London Bridge station. It held twenty-six passengers; fourteen on the top
deck and twelve inside. Each bus company was distinguished by its colour;
the Paddington bus was yellow and ran from Bank via Holborn, Oxford
Street, Edgware Road, and Harrow Road to the Royal Oak at Harlesden.
The fare was fourpence for the whole trip and buses ran every five minutes.
The horses did two trips as a day's work and were changed once each trip.

84
Hokey pokey stall, c.1887

The hot weather on Jubilee Day brought good business to the ice cream sellers. Known as 'hokey pokey', the ice creams were made in very unhygienic conditions. However, the five ragged boys here appear to be enjoying their penny treat.

85
Milk delivery, c.*1887*

The cart carried a seventeen-gallon churn and a four-gallon hand can. The milk cost fourpence a quart and was poured into pewter cans kept hanging on hooks at the tradesmen's entrance to the house. The milk roundsman also sold cream in little brown earthenware jugs, with paper tops tied on with string.

86
Fish stall, c.*1887*

Fish was regularly hawked around the streets of London, and the cart seen here is typical. The wooden cask holds the fish, which had been packed in ice and the straw seen on the cart. The fish are cut up or filleted, as requested by the customer, on the cutting board at the back. A little bit of fish was a popular Victorian tea-time delicacy.

87 Right
The chimney sweep, c.*1887*

London at the time of the Jubilee suffered from severe fogs because of the large number of coal fires. In the summer months chimney sweeps were kept busy preparing the chimneys for winter. The familiar brush seen in the photograph was invented in 1802 by George Smart, together with the hollow extending rods. In 1887 it cost five shillings to have a complete set of chimneys cleaned.

88 Left
Match seller, c.1887

The little boy without shoes is selling matches called 'Bryant and May's Alpine Vesuvians'. These were long slow-burning fuse matches, costing one penny for a box of twenty. Safety matches were introduced by the company in 1862, and were much cheaper at six boxes for a penny.

89
Crockery stall, c.1887

Two young men are selling plain white household crockery outside Swigg's Hotel in Greenwich. The cups, saucers, plates and pots are wrapped in straw. The coster barrow could be hired by the day, so crockery might only be today's line, depending on what bargain the two entrepreneurs found at the market place. The lady with the basket is selling lavender sachets to place in clothes and drawers.

90
Rabbit seller, c.*1887*

The rabbits were caught and brought into London from the then rural outskirts such as Bromley, Eltham or Bexley Heath. They cost sixpence each and were a good buy for the poorer classes, whose diet often consisted solely of bread and potatoes. As well as rabbits the poor could buy the scraps from the large joints trimmed by butchers, who would often give leftover pieces away on Saturday nights.

91
Ginger cakes for sale, c.*1887*

A street vendor of this Victorian delicacy stands in the road offering his wares, with a paper bag at the ready to wrap the cakes. In poor districts a considerable amount of food was available from street vendors, especially at weekends, on Bank Holidays, and for special occasions such as the Jubilee. Midday or midnight, the street vendors were there.

92 Left
General Viscount Wolseley, 1887

He entered the army in 1852, fought in the Indian Mutiny of 1857, in China in 1860, and put down the Canadian Red River rebellion in 1870, without losing a man. He defeated the Ashanti of West Africa in the war of 1873/74, and in 1881 defeated the Egyptian insurgents. Because of the hesitancy of Prime Minister Gladstone he was unable to rescue General Gordon at Khartoum in 1882. A popular figure, he commanded the troops at the Jubilee Review at Aldershot.

93 Right
Robert Cecil, Marquess of Salisbury, 1887

Lord Salisbury was Prime Minister at the time of Queen Victoria's Jubilee. He had been elected in the previous year to head a Conservative Government, allied with the Liberal Unionists. He became Prime Minister again in 1895, and in 1900. He was chiefly conspicuous as Foreign Secretary, an office that he combined with the premiership for many years.

94 Left
The Honourable William Ewart Gladstone, 1887

Leader of the Liberal Party who were in opposition at the time of the Jubilee. He began his politcal career as a Tory, but joined the ranks of the Whigs after the death of Lord Palmerston. He remained a Liberal for thirty years until his death in 1898.

95 Right
Lord Randolph Spencer Churchill, 1887

This active and adventurous politician was elected Conservative Member of Parliament for Woodstock in 1874. At thirty-six he was the youngest ever Chancellor of the Exchequer, under Lord Salisbury, but he resigned in 1886 over the expenditure on armaments. He was at this time Leader of the Conservative Party in the House of Commons, as the Prime Minister had to sit in the House of Lords.

96 Left
Lady Randolph Churchill, 1887

An American by birth and the daughter of a millionaire, Jennie Jerome was a great beauty and society hostess of her day. She married Lord Randolph in 1874, and their son was Sir Winston Spencer Churchill, KG.

97 Right
Lillie Langtry, 1887

Lillie Langtry was called the Jersey Lily after her birthplace. A poor actress, but a great beauty of her day and a friend of kings and princes, she moved in the highest circles of society. She dressed in the height of fashion and introduced the long-sleeved close-fitting 'jersey', knitted from silk or wool.

98
Buffalo Bill and British policemen, 1887

Buffalo Bill is in the centre of this group at Earl's Court, Kensington, the showground for his circus. Police Superintendent Fisher sits on his right, and on the extreme right in the feathered head-dress stands the Sioux Chief Red Shirt. Queen Victoria enjoyed the show so much that she insisted on seeing it again. A Royal Command Performance was arranged at Windsor Castle on the day before the Jubilee, for all her guests.

99
Policemen at Taunton, 1887

The police constables line up in their new uniforms. The familiar helmets have no badges and they are not wearing the leather belts, on which were hung the truncheon in a leather case and the bull's eye lantern. In 1887 the truncheon was carried in a large pocket in the trousers, where it is still carried today.

100 Right
Police constables

These policemen are from the Metropolitan Police Force, which was in charge of controlling the vast crowds and heavy traffic on the day of the Jubilee. They were highly commended by the public and press for their efforts. The helmets are similar to those worn today and were first issued in 1865. The helmet plate has the imperial crown adopted by Queen Victoria after Her Majesty had been proclaimed Empress of India. In the centre are the constable's letter and number, which correspond with those on his collar. The whistle was adopted in 1884, as the old-fashioned rattle could not be heard above the roar of London traffic.

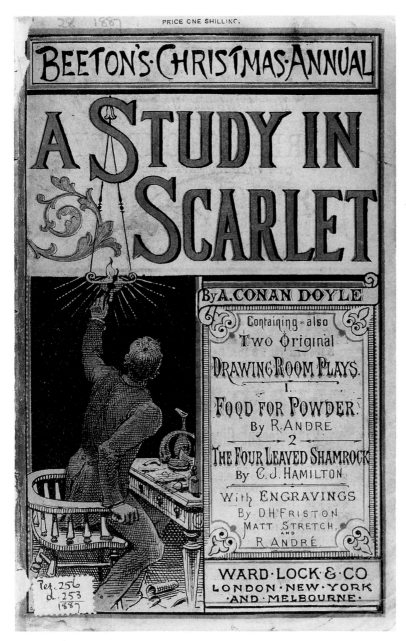

101
Beeton's Christmas Annual, 1887

The first appearance of the master detective Sherlock Holmes was in Beeton's Christmas Annual in the Jubilee year. Dr A. Conan Doyle established himself as a general practitioner at Southsea in 1882, and it was here that the first Sherlock Holmes story was written. The Doctor received £25 for this first story. This rare copy of the magazine is now worth a four-figure sum to collectors.